# THE AUTHORITY GUIDE TO
# CREATING BRAND STORIES THAT SELL

Smart and simple strategies to make your business irresistible

## JIM O'CONNOR

**The Authority Guide to Creating Brand Stories that Sell**

Smart and simple strategies to make your business irresistible

© Jim O'Connor

ISBN 978-1-909116-99-3
eISBN 978-1-912300-01-3

Published in 2017 by Authority Guides
authorityguides.co.uk

Printed in the United Kingdom.

# Contents

Great brands are the ones that tell the best stories. Sure, good products and services matter, but stories are what connect people with companies.

**Jason Fried**
**founder of Basecamp**

# Introduction

So, you are interested in creating brand stories and marketing messages that will prove irresistibly attractive to potential customers.

Me too. As a professional copywriter I've helped huge numbers of very different businesses rise to this challenge – from big consumer brands like Colgate-Palmolive, Heinz and Dairy Crest to small engineering companies, software developers and boutique hotels. What's more, unlike most copywriters, and indeed most people in marketing, I've been employed in sales. Face to face with real prospects you quickly receive short sharp lessons in what they want to hear, and what they don't.

I'm not telling you this to blow my own trumpet, just to reassure you that I have gained some valuable experience and knowledge.

Why do I want to share this now? Because I see so many businesses, full of great people giving it their all, making a horrible mess of presenting their offering to potential customers.

Instead of preparing their brand story in a systematic and strategic fashion they just dive in and start kicking ideas around. Rather than asking sensible preliminary questions like 'What's our offering?', 'How does it differ from that of our competitors?' and 'What do potential customers most want to hear?' they skip straight to 'We need a website', 'Let's do AdWords' and 'We must get busy on social media.' They start discussing *how* to communicate their message before first working out *what* it should be.

This is a sure-fire way to create chaos.

An old man is walking along a beach. He sees a boy at the waterline who is saving stranded starfish by throwing them back into the sea. The old man says, 'What's the point? There are so many – you'll never make a difference.' The boy throws back another and replies, 'I just made a difference to that one!' Over the years I've made a difference to many businesses, one at a time. But now I'd like to try and make a difference to larger numbers.

In this book I share a simple, practical and proven process for preparing a brand story that works – one that says the right things, to the right people, in the right order and in the right way for maximum impact. It's less about how to write and more about how to think.

If you are frustrated that your marketing is not producing the results you'd like, and worried that your brand story is too weak to punch its way out of a wet paper bag, then this little book will be a big help.

# 1. Key insights before we start the process

Let's begin by getting in the right frame of mind. In this chapter I share a few ideas and principles that will prove helpful.

## What is a brand?

Everyone is familiar with the brand word but I think it means very different things to different people.

Personally, I like this definition, proposed by Robert Jones, teacher at the University of East Anglia, and strategist at leading brand consultancy Wolff Olins. I'll paraphrase it here: A brand is a set of ideas a company or product stands for in people's minds. These ideas are shaped by the actions of that company or those products. But they are also given recognisable shape and form through the words and visual style the company and product uses to express itself.

If you buy into this definition you accept that a brand is not a single fixed entity. It is multifarious, intangible and ever-changing – it exists in the mind as a collection of impressions, perceptions and feelings. These are partly created by what the company or product says about itself, the story it chooses to tell people and the marketing messages it decides to communicate.

The key question, for you and your brand, is what story you propose telling. What should you include, what should you leave out and what is the best way to shape it?

## Why isn't my marketing working?

If you're confused by marketing in general, and frustrated by your own efforts in particular, then you are not alone. Marketing has never been simple or easy – and now is even less so. Like so much else, it has been turned upside down by the digital revolution. New technology promised to make things easier and the process more cost-effective. In many ways it has had the opposite effect.

- New media and clever targeting tools mean customers have become punch-drunk with information. To retain their sanity they've turned off, tuned out and retreated behind personal firewalls, both digital and mental. In theory people may be easier to reach but in practice they're harder to engage.

- Life is so fast paced and full on that people simply don't have the time or brain space to get excited about whatever it is you are promoting.

- Most people have virtually everything they need – car, smartphone and dishwasher. Every market, from professional services to potato products, is jam-packed with virtually indistinguishable offerings desperately vying for attention from people who are spoilt for choice and suffering from decision fatigue.

- Marketing has become more complicated and fragmented. There's such a profusion of new channels, tools and techniques that it's impossible to keep up – if you are struggling, then you are in good company!

To overcome these challenges a brand needs a very simple story which immediately strikes the target audience as relevant, meaningful, engaging, motivating and memorable. Creating such a story is a very demanding task, one that requires time and effort.

Despite this obvious truth, and the fact that 'brand story telling' is a term that has become very popular, a lot of business owners, managers and marketers are focused elsewhere – the message is the very last thing on their minds. Their attention is directed almost exclusively towards three other areas:

- Media – look at all these new ways to reach people! Let's try AdWords, pay-per-click, a website refresh, videos, retargeting ads, content marketing, an email campaign, our own app, Google+, LinkedIn, affiliate marketing…

- Mechanics – how do we get the best out of all these new tools and techniques? Let's learn more about search engine optimisation (SEO), getting likes and shares, MailChimp, proximity marketing, Vimeo, automation, QR codes, purpose-driven marketing, WordPress, user experience (UX), infographics, whiteboard animation…

- Metrics – if we measured more we could improve our effectiveness. Let's get busy monitoring views, like and shares, click rates, bounce rates, customer retention rates, lead quality scores, subscriber numbers, retention statistics, customer lifetime value…

These three things are getting lots of attention, because they are new and exciting. And they *are* important. But at the same time you cannot afford to ignore the fourth 'M' – message. What you say is at least as important as how you deliver it, how you amplify it and how you measure it. Doing a great job of broadcasting, augmenting and evaluating a rubbish message is a very expensive waste of time and effort.

Yet this is exactly what's happening. The words, the message, the story, are now dismissively described as 'content'. Why? Because with so many marketing projects it's only at the very end, when everything else has been put in place, that someone notices that the template is empty. The 'Where's the content?' question is very much an afterthought – at which point a copy-writer like myself is invited to 'fill it up'.

Am I exaggerating? No – many businesses, and the marketing professionals they hire, see nothing wrong with this approach. I'm repeatedly shocked at the number of times I've asked 'What do you want to say and what information can you give me?' only to receive a blank look or a reply that suggests I'm being difficult. A few years ago I was writing a major report for an international non-governmental organisation (NGO) based in Geneva. When I requested more information the reply was 'Your business is called "Stories that sell", can't you just make something up to fill the gaps?' They weren't joking, and were unamused when I replied that 'I only do non-fiction.'

## Words are cheap

I recently wrote a simple website for a financial services start-up. When the client involved an SEO consultancy they quoted £5,000 a month and insisted on a 12-month contract. Their monthly fee was almost ten times my one-off cost. The client eventually accepted another quote of £300 a week, £1,200 a month – still twice my fee, and not payable once, but 12 times a year. This shows you how little value, relatively speaking, is placed on the message itself.

So, concerned that your marketing isn't working as well as you'd like? Ask yourself whether you have become so absorbed by media, mechanics and metrics that you've dropped the message ball. And, if you suspect this is the case, how can you begin to put things right?

## It's about people – duh!

How have marketers got themselves into this pickle? It's because the industry is obsessed with novelty. The latest generation of practitioners believes that in today's brave new digital world the old ways of doing things are entirely redundant.

This attitude is foolish. Sir Isaac Newton remarked 'If I have seen further, it is by standing on the shoulders of giants.' And he got that line from Bernard of Chartres, writing in the 12th century. The point being that, even if times have changed, there might still be something to be learnt from those who have gone before. And that if you are ignorant of the past you'll probably waste a lot of time and energy, while feeling pretty pleased with yourself, reinventing the wheel!

The attitude is also misguided. The world has moved on but the job itself is still essentially the same. Marketing, as Stephen Leacock remarked almost a century ago, is the process 'of arresting human intelligence long enough to get money from it'. This is as true now as it was then. What's more, human nature is no different from what it was before the arrival of Microsoft, Apple, Google and Facebook. Go even further back, to the time of Shakespeare, or of the ancient Greeks or Romans, and you'll find we're fundamentally little changed. So, the job of marketing is essentially the same – we're just working with slightly more modern tools.

This novelty-obsessed mindset is also very unhelpful. It prioritises technology over psychology. Given that marketing is about encouraging people to part with cash, you ignore the workings of the human mind at your peril!

## Words of wisdom about what it takes to win hearts and minds

Some smart people have long understood that successful marketing is more art than science:

> There are a lot of great technicians in advertising. And unfortunately they talk the best game. They know all the rules. They can tell you that people in an ad will get you greater readership. They can tell you that a sentence should be this short or that long. They can tell you that body copy should be broken up for easier reading. They can give you fact after fact after fact. They are the scientists of advertising. But there's one little rub. Advertising is fundamentally persuasion and persuasion happens to be not a science, but an art. (Dobrow, 1984)

Bill Bernbach wrote that in 1947. It was true then, and it's true now, because people have not fundamentally changed.

Fundamentals *don't* change. That makes them boring. Clever people (especially those keen to be seen as such) tend to overlook fundamentals. Wise people don't.

So, if you want your marketing to work, remember the fundamentals. Don't let the new technology, tools and techniques seduce you into ignoring good old psychology, persuasion and enticement – understanding human needs, wants and fears is every bit as important as being a whizz with WordPress, retargeting and multi-channel analytics.

## Let me tell you all about me, me, me

You don't have to study Sigmund Freud or Carl Jung to create persuasive marketing messages – a basic understanding of practical psychology is quite sufficient.

I've always been good at getting on with people. So when someone suggested I would be a more successful sales person if I read *How to Win Friends and Influence People* I smiled to myself – *I* don't need to read a book like *that*, I told myself! However, when I read a copy I was shocked to make a couple of discoveries. There were things, important things, that I didn't know I didn't know. And it dawned on me that you don't have to be bad at something to get better.

The key point in the book is this simple truth – all of us are primarily interested in ourselves. We're all programmed to be self-centred, self-absorbed and self-interested.

So, when I or you promote something, our natural inclination is to talk about ourselves, our experience, our skills, our products and our services.

What's wrong with that? Everything! Because the person we are trying to engage, to win over, to influence, is not interested in *any* of that stuff. They don't care. They, like us, are totally wrapped up in themselves, their problems, their hopes, their needs, their fears. The thing they most want to hear about, the subject that is guaranteed to get their attention, is themselves.

## A simple experiment that proves the point

Have you ever been cornered at a business networking event by someone who won't shut up about themselves and never asks a question about you? Then you've experienced for yourself what a turn-off it is. And have you ever tried the reverse tactic yourself – refusing to talk about yourself and always switching the conversation back to the other person? Give it a go and you'll suddenly find people a lot happier to share your company. What's more, at some point in the conversation most of them will reciprocate and start to ask questions about you.

The surest way to get people interested in you and what you have to say is to show that kind of interest in them first. But how can this be applied when it comes to your brand story and sales messages? There's a simple formula that smart marketers use, developed many years ago, drawing on the same insights as Dale Carnegie.

## Features and benefits – what's the difference?

Most business people claim to be familiar with the concept of features and benefits – but surprisingly few apply it in practice with much degree of consistency or effectiveness.

A feature is a fact about your product or service. It might be 'We've been in business over 20 years', or 'We provide online access to your account' or 'Our detergent is concentrated.' Features are essential if you are constructing a believable brand story or sales message. Without features you are merely creating fiction – who is going to believe you if you don't give them facts?

However, facts are not enough. If *all* you give people are facts they are likely to respond with 'So what?' because they are self-interested – people want to know what's in it for *them*. Features are considerably more powerful when coupled with the corresponding benefit.

## Features and benefits – some examples

Feature: We are a pet-friendly hotel.
Benefit: You don't have to leave your four-legged friends at home when you travel, plus you save on kennel and cattery fees.

Feature: We provide cash flow solutions to small to medium-sized enterprises (SMEs).
Benefit: No more waiting 30, 60 or 90 days to get paid, so the financial pressure is off.

Feature: Online access to your account.
Benefit: Convenience – check balances and conduct transactions from anywhere in the world, any time you like, 24/7.

Feature: We've been in business over 20 years.
Benefit: Peace of mind that we are experienced and have the knowledge and skills required to solve your problem.

Feature: Our detergent is very concentrated.
Benefit: Takes up less storage space, makes your shopping bag easier to carry and is more environmentally friendly because trucks transporting bottles with a higher water content use more fuel and create more emissions.

It's therefore common sense to always present your features with their corresponding benefits – ideally with the benefit coming first and the feature second. Think of it like a horse and cart. The benefit is the part of the message with the pulling power, so it works best when you put it up front!

However, look around at most marketing collateral, from websites to ads and brochures to eshots, and you'll see common sense is not common. Business owners and marketers just can't resist leading with features, features and more features. There might be the occasional benefit but generally it's buried, or at least it comes a poor second.

## How *not* to do it

Let's imagine this is the text on the home page of a website.

**Mobile cocktail bar hire service**

**We provide full mobile cocktail bar hire solutions for any event and pride ourselves on delivering exceptional customer service – from Plymouth to Newcastle and London to Manchester plus all points in between. Your mobile bar includes all the cocktail essentials such as bar equipment hire, glassware hire, and the choice of a fully stocked and staffed bar or a dry bar option. A wide range of styles is available – vintage mobile cocktail bar hire, American-style bar hire or the modern Italian LED mobile cocktail bar hire.**

This text is all features – fact after fact. It's informative (and there's nothing wrong with that). However, it's not very engaging, exciting or motivating. Giving the detail, without the benefits, risks getting the 'So what?' reaction – there's room for improvement.

## A better way to do it

**Mobile cocktail bar hire – we mix drinks, you mix with your guests**

**Playing host is hard work – so leave the planning, preparation, mixing and serving to us, while you get on and party! We offer a range of stylish mobile bar hire packages that can be customised to suit any venue. A wide choice of colours, configurations and themes means we won't cramp your style! We can provide all mainstream drinks, including real ales, draught lagers and soft drinks – everything to break the ice and shake things up in style!**

This text leads with benefits. It immediately tells the reader what's in it for them – less preparation, less work and less stress, plus more fun for everyone. Having hooked the reader in by appealing to their self-interest, and talking directly about things that are personally relevant, you can then start going into the detail without fear of losing them.

Why do so many people make the classic mistake of focusing on features whilst forgetting the benefits? Because they are programmed to talk about themselves. They just want to 'get our company name across', to 'increase our brand awareness' and 'establish our credentials'. Fine, but the name is meaning-less, the brand irrelevant and the credentials of no interest, until the customer knows what's in it for them.

So, if you want your brand story or marketing message to have power and traction the focus should be on the prospect rather than on you. It has to say something meaningful and motivating to them, with the benefit up big and up front. Check the front cover of this book – the title and the subtitle both have benefits in them. The first line of the introduction – it's about you, the reader.

> ### Key points to take away
>
> - Your brand is largely shaped by the kind of story you choose to tell about it.
>
> - Don't put so much focus on media, mechanics and metrics that you neglect the all-important message.
>
> - Remember the fundamental fact that marketing hasn't changed as much as you might imagine – it's still about people, and human nature is the same as it ever was.
>
> - The best way to attract people is to talk about their favourite subject – themselves.
>
> - Make the features of your offering more relevant and appealing by always presenting them with an accompanying benefit.

# 2. List your features and benefits

The features are the basic raw material for your brand story and marketing messages – so the best way to start preparing what you should say is by simply getting *all* of them out on the table.

I stress the word all because it's important not to be selective at this stage. Don't judge them, don't weigh up one against another, don't worry about whether the competitors offer something similar and don't fret about which will resonate the most with the target audience – right now you just need to have a brain dump!

## Work from the inside out

You might like to begin with your more intangible features, those that relate to values, principles, culture, vision and sense of purpose. Essentially you are defining what's at the heart of your brand and asking 'What do we stand for?'

This type of self-analysis has become increasingly popular, with a growing consensus that companies and products with a clear sense of purpose, one that goes beyond merely making a profit, tend to be viewed more favourably by consumers. The Body Shop helped pioneer this approach but has been joined by the likes of Dove (on a mission to raise the self-esteem of girls and women), Nike (on a mission to bring inspiration and innovation to every athlete in the world; note: *everybody* is an athlete), Apple (on a mission to empower creative exploration and self-expression) and Starbucks (on a mission to inspire and nurture the human spirit one person, one cup, at a time), to name but a few.

We now see a huge number of companies, organisations and brands placing great emphasis on value statements, mission statements and vision statements. These are the basic building blocks which sit at the heart of purpose-driven organisations and brands.

## Purpose – a cautionary note

Whilst not denying the obvious merits of including these features I would make a couple of caveats.

First, not all products and brands are purpose driven – at least not in the sense of having a *higher* purpose, of making the world a better place and giving back to society. Let's say you run a small craft brewery or a software development company, a shopfitting business or a training consultancy. You've probably got your hands full already without taking on some much bigger and more altruistic mission.

What's more, if your highest goal is to give your customers great products and services, so you can pay the mortgage and take the occasional holidays, there's nothing wrong with that. If you are good at what you do, and treat people well, then that's probably sufficient. It's only if you want to take over the world that you have to promise you'll make it better in the process!

Second, being recognised as a purpose-driven brand is not enough. A mission statement, vision statement, a values statement and an intent to 'do good' are all laudable, but they tend to be rather inward looking. Furthermore, the consumer, as we noted earlier, is primarily self-interested. They may be unimpressed by the fact that you're on a mission to end exploitation, promote fair trade or save the rainforest. Just look at how many times consumers discover that brands are behaving badly but remain loyal simply because the price is right or they can't be bothered to switch.

So, for a brand story or marketing message to be really effective you also need to consider those features that are more outwardly directed and tangible. For instance, what products or services do you offer, what are their key characteristics, how do you make these available, what's the pricing structure, what sectors of the market do you specialise in, are you members of any trade associations, what relevant accreditations do you hold, what warranties are available, what are the payment terms, what value-added services are included?

## Now the benefits

Once you're happy you've itemised every possible feature go back and put yourself in the prospect's shoes – view these features from their perspective. Take one at a time and ask 'So what?' List the answer alongside the feature as I did with the examples in the previous chapter. That way you'll be clear on how to make each individual feature meaningful and motivating for your prospects.

## Key points to take away

- List *all* the features you can think of.

- Don't forget the intangible and internal features relating to your mission, values and vision – what you stand for.

- Also include the tangible and external features – what you offer.

- Think of the benefit that goes with each of the features on your list.

# 3. Understand your target audience

You now have a full list of features and benefits. But which of these should be given most prominence in your brand story or marketing messages? You've described the benefits as you see them, but perhaps the target audience has an entirely different view? You are clear on what you want to say – but is this what potential customers most want to hear?

The next stage is to list *all* those people who are likely to be interested in what you have to offer. I say *all* because you may have one offering but a buying process that involves several decision makers or influencers. Or, you may have multiple offerings that appeal to a very diverse range of different consumers. List all these buyers and influencers, defining them in simple terms so it's clear who you are seeking to influence.

## One buyer or more?

- If you are selling beer you're probably aiming to influence a single customer – the person who drinks it.

- With items like bread, fruit juice or yoghurt you may be selling to a family – who has the biggest say in the decision, mum, dad or the kids?

- If you are in a business-to-business (B2B) market the decision may involve executives from information technology (IT) to production, finance to human resources (HR), purchasing to the chief executive officer (CEO).

- Some companies provide multiple offerings to a variety of buyers. I have worked for a retailer of outdoor clothing and equipment who identified over 30 different types of potential buyers, from the serious mountaineer to the retired couple walking the dog, and the gadget freak that can't resist the latest technology to the gym enthusiast seeking out the trendiest athleisure brands.

If you are in a situation where several people are involved in the purchasing decision, or where you have multiple offerings for a variety of buyers, you will have to produce a number of different variants to your story. You'll need one overarching version that is broad enough to appeal to the entire target audience (to go on the home page of your website, for instance). You'll also need other versions that talk directly to each subgroup of buyers (an email to the serious mountaineers, an email to the dog walkers and so on).

Once you have completed the list you might have something like 'owner-managers of small businesses with up to five employees within 50 miles of Bristol', or 'mums aged 20-45 with kids in the ABC1 socio-economic demographic' or 'retired couples/empty nesters aged 50+ with a household income of £50,000+ that take more than one foreign holiday a year'.

Now it's time to flesh out those brief descriptions.

- What problems do they have that you could solve?
- What are their hopes and fears, needs and wants?

- What do they most want to hear when looking for the kind of product or service you are offering?

- How important is price to them, or quality or choice or personal service or expert advice or a money-back guarantee?

- Do these people have particular attitudes that will affect how they view your offering? A distrust of all finance providers or a fondness for all things organic, for instance?

You need to get into their head and heart to understand what it is that motivates them, and why.

## Head versus heart

In 1943 psychologist Abraham Maslow introduced what has become known as 'Maslow's Hierarchy of Needs'.

Figure 1 Maslow's Hierarchy of Needs

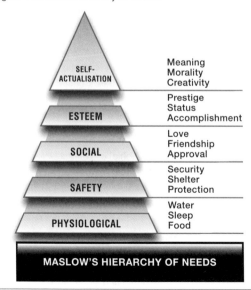

This is represented as a pyramid, with our most basic physical and practical needs at the bottom. The idea is that as we satisfy one level of needs we progress to the next. Moving up, we become more concerned with emotional needs, finally reaching the very top where our needs are more spiritual.

So, for instance, when we stop worrying about being cold and hungry we fret about our safety. Once we feel safe we look for love and friendship – we have a need to be accepted and to 'belong'. Once we have successfully fitted in we develop aspirations to stand out, for others to look up to us. We worry less about how others see us and become more interested about how we see ourselves – we're driven by the urge to fulfil our potential, to express ourselves and to enjoy rewarding experiences. At the very pinnacle we are most concerned with our spiritual needs, pursuing goals that are bigger than ourselves.

Whether you entirely agree with this model it does point to the fact that humans have very complex and evolving needs. A marketer that concentrates entirely on logical, tangible and practical benefits, but ignores the social, emotional and spiritual ones, is underselling their offering.

Let's take a very simple example. The first benefit that comes to mind with a high-performance jacket will be something like 'protects you from the elements in extreme conditions but has excellent breathability and wicks away sweat when you are exerting yourself'. However, there will be another group that buys it for totally different reasons – they want to look like an adventurous type when stood on the touchline at their son's rugby match. Focus exclusively on the practical benefits and you could miss all those who are more concerned with status and self-image.

Those businesses that develop the best understanding of what their consumers want are most successful at attracting them – Amazon, Lush, Apple and Uber spring to mind. Big companies like these spend a fortune gathering consumer insights to gain competitive advantage. Small businesses cannot make the same investment – but they can still gain valuable insights by other means.

- Forget about yourself and your objectives. Put yourself in your customer's situation and try to imagine how they think and feel (abandon all your assumptions!).

- Ask yourself, 'If I was them, looking at us, what factors are most likely to influence their decision – what do they most want to hear?'

- If you don't have close contact with prospects and customers then talk to your salespeople – find out what messages they feel are most effective, what objections they most regularly encounter and what insights they can add.

- Talk to real customers and ask what's important to them – you could phone a few, organise focus groups, maybe invite them to give online feedback, or attend trade shows to observe and question them.

- Read – you can glean valuable insights from articles in business magazines and trade publications, industry association reports, white papers, blogs and customer review sites.

The better you understand the mentality of the target audience the clearer picture you will have of the person you want to influence. This in turn improves your chances of creating a brand story and marketing messages they'll find engaging and persuasive. You are more likely to click with someone if you know what makes them tick!

## Key points to take away

- List *all* those involved in the buying decision for your products and services.

- Create a detailed pen portrait of each individual type of person on your list – this is known as developing personas.

- Ask what these different groups most want to hear from you. (What are their logical, tangible and practical needs, as well as their social, emotional and spiritual ones?)

- The better you understand your prospects the greater your chances of creating a brand story that appeals to them.

# 4. Analyse your competition

The next step is to identify your main competitors and how your offering lines up alongside theirs.

Start by listing your *closest* competition. If you run a craft brewery you are technically competing against all the other breweries in the UK (over 1,000 of them), against all those foreign brewers who export to this country and even against all the ciders, wines and spirits available. However, listing all these is pointless – focus on the half dozen other beers most similar to yours that are most readily available and popular in your core marketing area.

Next, take these competitors, one by one, and compare their offering to yours. Do this by listing their most significant product or service features (as you did for your own offering), covering everything from their pricing structure to their distribution model and their packaging to their current marketing activity. The idea is to identify their strengths and weaknesses relative to your own and try to find a 'gap in the market' that you can exploit to your advantage.

The most systematic way to do this is with a strengths, weaknesses, opportunities, threats (SWOT) analysis. This is a simple but useful framework for analysing your company's strengths and weaknesses, and the opportunities and threats that it faces (Figure 2).

Figure 2 SWOT analysis template

**STRENGTHS**
What are the best points about our business?

**WEAKNESSES**
What are the worst points about our business?

**SWOT**

**OPPORTUNITIES**
What external situations can we exploit to our advantage?

**THREATS**
What external factors could cause us problems?

Once you've completed this exercise the information will form the basis for further discussion and is a great starting point for formulating strategy. It might highlight that you are weak on new product development and need to put more effort into this activity. It might reveal that there is an opportunity to grow your business by investing in a particular new technology. You might discover that you are in a sufficiently strong position to raise your prices. Finally, it might alert you to new regulation requiring a change in the way you approach prospects.

The SWOT analysis helps with all areas of business planning and strategy, but it is obviously very useful when trying to create the most effective brand stories and sales messages. It clarifies where you are currently positioned in the marketplace, and influences what kind of things you should be saying. It may even identify a meaningful point of difference between you and your immediate competitors.

The word meaningful is important – the point of difference needs to have some kind of value for the prospect. You might be the longest established solicitors in Somerset but who, apart from yourselves, cares? It *is* a difference, but what difference does it *make*? However, if you are the only solicitors in the South West whose family law team includes a surrogacy specialist, then that *is* meaningful – it makes a difference to people who have a surrogacy issue or want advice on that subject, as well as suggesting that your family law expertise is more extensive than that of competitors.

## How your positioning helps shape your story

I've worked with a leading retailer of outdoor clothing and equipment. They have about 75 stores across the UK and a big ecommerce site. Their main competitor is similar in this regard – but very different in other ways.

The company I helped has traditional shops on the high street while the other sells from huge sheds on out-of-town retail parks. The first tends to stock the better known, high-quality, premium-price brands like The North Face, Berghaus, Columbia, Helly Hansen and Rab. The other sells a more limited range of premium brands plus a lot of lower-priced products from the likes of Freedom Trail, Dare2b, Regatta and The Edge. The in-store experience is also different, with the first relatively upmarket and the other very much discount shopping.

Given these facts I worked with my client to create a brand story and sales messages that stressed value over price. We suggested that better quality products last longer and that the cheap option will probably cost more in the long run. We also created a narrative around the idea that kit you can trust to perform well and keep you comfortable, even in the most extreme conditions, is worth every penny – it makes the whole experience of being outdoors, whether that's just walking the dog or climbing Mount Everest, so much more rewarding and satisfying.

The competitor's story was also shaped by their positioning. It was less about how high-performance kit enhances your enjoyment of the outdoors and more about fun, savings and discounts. Their keyword, and one they used repeatedly, was 'WOW'. For them the wow factor was their amazing prices. For my client the wow factor (although they never used the word they did express it through the imagery) was the amazing locations and experience you can enjoy when you have kit you can trust.

When you know where you are positioned it's a lot easier to decide what kind of story you need to tell.

### Key points to take away

- Make a list of your closest competitors.
- Conduct a SWOT analysis to clarify your position in the marketplace.
- The SWOT analysis will help you to shape a story that makes you stand out from the crowd.

# 5. Decide on your proposition

Up to this point we've been accumulating information. Now we need to start distilling it. This stage is akin to creating a powerful spirit such as whisky or vodka – you boil off almost everything until all that's left is a concentrated product with a high alcohol content that's really intoxicating. It's the same with a brand. You reduce the information until you are left with just the essence, a powerful promise that exerts a strong influence on consumers.

## How do you distil your information?

Start by looking at your features, and the benefits they offer. Next, place them side by side with what the target audience wants to hear, the benefits that most appeal to them. The area where they overlap is where you need to start digging for a promise that'll prove relevant and motivating to your prospects.

Next, use your SWOT analysis to bring the competitor's offering into the equation. Your rivals will probably cover some of the same features and benefits as you. It's likely they'll also be saying things that have a strong consumer appeal. Hopefully, however, there will still be some area of connection between you and your prospects where your competitors are relatively weak – where you have that meaningful point of difference we touched on earlier. This is the 'sweet spot' where your best promise is to be found. Figure 3 should help you to visualise what I'm describing.

Figure 3 The brand story sweet spot

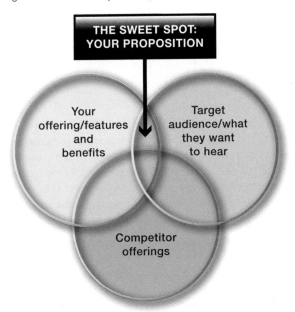

At this point you'll either be thinking 'Wonderful, we have a meaningful point of difference we can exploit', or 'Oh dear, we don't!' If it's the former then coming up with a good proposition will be a bit easier. If it's the latter then don't worry – in today's hypercompetitive world it's not an uncommon situation, nor is it insurmountable.

## The unique selling proposition myth

'Find your USP' is a piece of advice that most business owners and marketing practitioners have probably heard before.

USP stands for unique selling proposition, a term coined by Rosser Reeves of Ted Bates & Company in the 1940s. He explained that a genuine USP 'Must be unique – either a uniqueness of the brand or a claim not otherwise made in that particular field of advertising' (Reeves, 2015). It was pedalled by his agency to differentiate themselves from a host of competitors – their USP was the fact they came up with the USP concept!

Way back then markets were less crowded, so the chances of being able to uncover or concoct a true USP were better. Today there are so many 'me-too' products and services, in every corner of every market, that trying to find a genuine USP is probably futile – show me the shampoo, consultant, yoghurt, SUV, bank, combi-drill, airline, mineral water or university that is genuinely unique. If you tried ridiculously hard you might be able to find some tiny point of difference that arguably makes you unique, but is it meaningful – does anyone, apart from you, care?

## Three characteristics of a good proposition

Let's assume you have a sweet spot, or at least an area where you are offering something that your audience wants (even if you are having to share it with rivals). How do you set about coming up with a great proposition?

First, remember that people are struggling with too much information, they are busy and stressed, and they don't have a lot of attention to spare. It's essential, therefore, that your promise is simple and single-minded.

Second, you must promise something you can genuinely deliver, but which the target audience desires. It should be motivating and exciting – the *most* motivating and exciting thing you can offer.

Third, it must be as differentiating as possible – although, as we've discussed, this may in practice be difficult to achieve. If you can find something that truly sets you apart, great. If you can't, you'll just have to do an excellent job of communicating what you *have* got.

Now, turn over all the information you have gathered in your mind, get a feel for what is most motivating and differentiating, and your promise will gradually start to take shape. The process will probably be easier to appreciate if I give you some examples.

### Examples of effective single-minded propositions

Boutique hotel: Our extraordinary personal service makes you feel more at home.

Decision support software: Gain valuable foresight sufficiently early to change outcomes for the better.

Retailer of quality outdoor equipment and clothing: Kit you can trust that lets you enjoy the outdoors to the max.

Invoice finance for SMEs: Grow your business faster by releasing the cash you have tied up in unpaid invoices.

Dog walking service: Enjoy a better dog/life balance.

Computer equipment disposal service: Complete peace of mind that your redundant equipment has been handled in a way that's totally compliant with the latest environmental and data security regulations.

Fruit juice: Tastes better because it's made exclusively from the finest Florida oranges.

Business consultancy: Our unique approach takes the pain out of growth.

Handmade pasta for busy commercial chefs: The finest handmade pasta delivered direct from Italy means you get the compliments without the hassle.

Document management service: Your organisation's precious documents are much safer being looked after by us.

The examples above are all simple and single-minded sentences. They also make the benefit clear – the target audience can immediately see what's in it for them and how they will gain. In some instances the promise also manages to differentiate itself from competitors.

## Key points to take away

Once you've gathered all the relevant raw material for your brand story you should distil it into a powerful proposition.

- Align the information about your offering, your target audience and your competitors to find the proposition sweet spot.

- Don't worry if you can't find a genuine USP – just concentrate on making the best promise you can.

- A good proposition is single-minded, motivating and differentiating.

Stories also create value. If you take a simple object and build a story around it, the value increases exponentially. People shop with their heads and their hearts, and they will pay for an object based on how much it means to them.

**Richelle Parham**
**former Chief Marketing Officer**
**for eBay**

# 6. Substantiate your proposition

People are naturally sceptical – and especially suspicious of claims made by marketers. So, you need to support your proposition with evidence that you can genuinely deliver.

This is where all that other material, the features and benefits, your understanding of the prospect's needs and wants, as well as your SWOT analysis, comes fully into play. However, these points have to be organised into a compelling argument. A bit like a barrister, your objective is to make a persuasive case that will sway the jury in the court of public opinion.

To do that you simply state your promise, then ask 'Why should anyone believe this?' Next, go through your lists and notes to find the points that answer this question and support the proposition. You'll soon assemble another list of bullet points all beginning with the word 'Because…'.

## Substantiation – an example

Promise: Your organisation's precious documents are much safer being looked after by us.

Substantiation:

- Because our document storage centre is surrounded by high and secure steel fencing

- Because access is only available through robust canti-lever gates controlled from our secure operations room

- Because the entire building is covered by state of the art 360° external and internal digital closed-circuit television (CCTV)

- Because we operate continuous wire and wire-free moni-toring of systems

- Because we have a direct link to the emergency services

- Because our building is fitted with a National Fire Protection Association sprinkler system – 8,000 sprinkler heads, installed at roof level, in every aisle and every rack

All of these points support the proposition, lend weight to the argument and help create a convincing case.

## Don't lose the plot

Not all the features and benefits on your list will be directly relevant to your proposition. For instance, in the example of the document management service, there will be other aspects of the offering that need to be included. As well as wanting to be reassured about the security systems, prospects will want to know about the process for handing over their archives in the first place, how they will be arranged and catalogued, how the database works, what type of boxes will be used, how the documents are moved to the secure facility and so on. They'll also want to know what kind of records management software is used, how the documents are retrieved and tracked, how much choice there is regarding delivery schedules and what proof of delivery mechanisms are in place.

These features and benefits are important, but supplementary to the main story about security and peace of mind. Obviously, they need to be included, but *after* the points that directly validate and underpin the primary promise. Your proposition provides you with a central organising principle – in the example featured here the security story is the primary one, and the points directly relating to that must be given priority. That's not to say that other elements cannot be included – they just come a little lower down the hierarchy.

It's the same with a well-constructed novel or film. There will be a hero, heroine or both, and some kind of challenge they are wrestling with – that's the main plot. However, there will always be subplots and supporting characters. These add weight and interest to the main narrative, but they are not allowed to hijack it – the primary focus is on the leading characters and the central plot.

So, coming up with a powerful promise is important in terms of grabbing the prospect's attention and engaging their interest. But it also helps you to create a clear story and messaging hierarchy. As Alvin Toffler remarked, 'You've got to think about big things while you're doing small things, so that all the small things go in the right direction' (Toffler, 1970).

## Key points to take away

Once you have decided on your proposition you need to convince prospects you can deliver on that promise.

- Rearrange your list of features and benefits to provide strong support for your proposition.

- A good brand story will have a main plot as well as several subplots.

- Those features and benefits that directly relate to your proposition become the main plot, those that don't are still included, but in the subplots.

It may well be that creativity is the last unfair advantage we're legally allowed to take over our competitors.

**Bill Bernbach**

# 7. It's time to get creative

Your brand story and marketing messages are now in pretty good shape. You're clear about what you should say, who you're talking to, what they want to hear, whether you have a meaningful point of difference you can exploit and the order in which you're going to deliver the main points.

However, you also need to be realistic – the challenges are considerable and your story has to be good, *really* good, if you are going to attract the attention of prospects and inch ahead of your competitors.

So, what can you do to achieve that? First you need to get in the right frame of mind, then grasp a couple of fundamental concepts about storytelling and marketing.

## Worried you'll be tuned out or squeezed out?

As we've already noted, people are suffering from a surfeit of information – they just don't have the bandwidth for all the stuff coming at them. Unless something immediately talks directly to them, about something they find particularly relevant or personally interesting, they ignore it. Attention is one of the rarest commodities in the world today.

So, is your brand story, and your marketing message, sufficiently powerful to penetrate the firewalls that surround your prospects? If you have your doubts, then don't despair – we'll look at some useful tips shortly.

A second challenge, as we've also noted, is that markets have never been more crowded or competitive. Whether you're an accountant or a therapist, selling handmade fudge or traditional farmhouse cider, offering marketing and design services or running a specialist employment agency, there'll be a bunch of others promoting something similar, exactly the same or even better. Ideally, you'll have a meaningful point of difference to help you stand out from the crowd. Most companies, however, are not in this happy position – and if that includes you then let me give you some hope.

You are concerned with being different, but how big an issue is this with consumers? They're busy, swamped with information and struggling with decision fatigue – if they find you and believe you can do a good job of solving their problem, meeting their need or satisfying their desire, then they'll probably go with you. Different is less important for them than the peace of mind that their crucial documents are safe, that your dog walking service means they can go for a drink straight from work without feeling guilty, or that your invoice finance facility enables them to get paid in 1 day rather than 30.

## Winning by the inch

All brands are facing these challenges to a greater or lesser degree. Even those with a meaningful point of difference will have rivals trying to erode that competitive advantage, and the challenge posed by switched-off consumers affects all marketers equally. So, *every* brand has to pull out all of the stops when it comes to engaging, motivating or seducing potential customers – the one that does it best wins!

How do you do that? There's no single, simple, definitive answer. But there are some insights and approaches that will help to make your brand story more attractive, engaging and persuasive.

Two hikers are going down a trail. Suddenly they encounter a big angry bear. One hiker swiftly pulls a pair of running shoes out of his pack and starts unlacing his heavy boots. The other hiker looks at him in amazement and says 'What are you doing? You'll never outrun a bear!' The other replies 'I don't have to outrun the bear. I just have to outrun *you*!' The point being you may be no better than your competitors, but there are little things you can do to pull ahead of them.

## Perception is everything

Don't let the reality of your competitive situation limit your thinking. The facts you have assembled whilst going through the process are just the starting point. The strategy document you are looking at now will be very different from the story you end up with.

We started this book by defining the meaning of the word brand as a set of ideas partly shaped by the reality of the products and services being offered and partly by the words and images used to express that reality. We noted that these ideas live in the minds of the many different people who become aware of the brand, each of which has their own individual perception of it. A brand is therefore a very fluid entity.

The reality is not irrelevant – but nor is it everything. If you promise something, then fail to deliver, or the experience is a huge disappointment, then that affects how the brand is perceived. Similarly, if your product or service is obviously inferior to that of your immediate competitors, then that is also bound to affect how people feel about it.

So, if you want to make your brand more competitive you may need to make some changes to the reality – enhance customer service, find ways to add value, invest in new machinery, lower your prices or whatever. Improving the reality should improve the perception. But once you've done that you are probably no more than level with the competition. Then what? If you want to get *ahead* of them the thing to work on is the perception itself.

Coca-Cola and Pepsi, Hertz and Avis, and Tesco and Sainsbury's are good examples of this. For many years they've worked on making the product and service itself as good as possible. And all they've achieved is parity – the differences between them are so negligible as to be meaningless. When one of those hire companies introduces driverless cars the other won't be far behind. That's why big brands spend so much time, money and effort on marketing: to create a more favourable *perception*.

The point is that if you have no meaningful point of difference and you are surrounded by competitors whose offerings are indistinguishable from yours, then it's not the end of the world. What matters is what you are going to do about it. And one of the most effective things you can do, maybe the *only* effective thing you can do, is to work on changing the way your brand is perceived.

Famous advertising creative Paul Arden wrote a bestseller entitled *It's Not How Good You Are, It's How Good You Want To Be*. It's about how to achieve success by thinking smarter and refusing to let the facts hold you back. That's exactly the attitude you need when building your brand in a way that stands out from the crowd. I'd just change the message to 'It's not how good you are, it's how good people think you are.'

The facts may say you are no better than the rest. But you *can* tell a better story. It's not about lying (don't – not only is it wrong, but you'll be found out). It's about presenting your offering in the best possible light, with the most engaging, interesting and persuasive story or message you can muster.

## It's the way that you tell them

There's a difference between a story and the way it is expressed – they are two separate entities. It's important to understand this, because the gap between them gives you a lot of room for manoeuvre. It's an opportunity to get creative and transform the story in your strategy document into something much more powerful and compelling.

Take the life of Christ. This story is told in the gospels of Matthew, Mark, Luke and John. It's the same life, the same story, but told four very different ways. Countless others have given us wildly divergent retellings (the Pauline Epistles, *The Da Vinci Code*, *The Testament of Mary*, *Ben Hur*, the *Life of Brian*…). The most dramatic incidents have also been expressed by artists who give us very different pictures. The Last Supper has most famously been painted by Leonardo da Vinci, but many others have given us alternative interpretations of the same scene (Tintoretto, Rubens, Andy Warhol, Tiepolo, Durer, Damien Hurst, Matthias Grünewald…).

Almost all of Shakespeare's plays are reworkings of much earlier stories – *Hamlet* is based on a Norse legend first written in Latin, *King Lear* on Raphael Holinshed's *Chronicles of England* and *A Midsummer Night's Dream* takes stories and characters from Ovid, Chaucer and Plutarch.

'Yesterday' by The Beatles has been covered by everyone from Shirley Bassey to Willie Nelson and Marianne Faithful to Tammy Wynette. Same song, same words, but a very different sound. Then there are movies and remakes, all of them different takes on the same basic story.

So, the story you start with is just that – a starting point. You can make of it what you will and take it in any direction you like. This is equally true of brand stories, so there's lots of room for creativity and imagination.

## The story of Volkswagen

Adolf Hitler wanted a cheap, simple car that could be mass-produced for his country's new road network. In 1934 he commissioned Ferdinand Porsche to design and build a 'people's car' and personally laid the cornerstone for the Volkswagen factory in Fallersleben. The Second World War disrupted production but in 1945 the British Army reopened the factory and started making military vehicles.

Given this story it was unlikely that the Volkswagen would become a bestseller in the US, a country that had sacrificed much to bring down the Nazi regime. The first VW Beetle arrived in 1949 and by 1970 had captured seven per cent of the US market, with annual sales peaking at 570,000 vehicles. This was an extraordinary achievement in a market extremely resistant to foreign imports.

Advertising agency Doyle Dane Bernbach successfully repositioned it as the car of choice for those who embraced the emergent counterculture of the 1960s. A vehicle originally developed by the Nazis, whose philosophies plunged the world into the biggest war of all time, became an icon for hippies espousing peace and love, as well as making it hugely popular with millions of the middle class. The company has had its ups and downs since then but at the start of 2017, despite landing itself in a major emissions scandal, the company was the largest car-maker in the world.

So, don't worry if the story you start out with isn't too promising. The way you tell it can make all the difference.

## Who is your hero?

Every story has a hero or heroine. So who is the star of your brand story – your company, your product, your service... or your customer? Most brands make the classic mistake we touched on earlier in the first chapter – they put the focus on themselves rather than on the person they are trying to attract.

## Spot the difference

Here's an example where the company has fallen into this trap.

**Established in 1987, Profit & Loss Accounting are an award-winning firm of accountants based in Wood End, specialising in the provision of expert practical and professional advice and assistance to business owners. Our experienced team offers a full range of services including taxation, payroll, VAT, staff pensions, business advice and help with cloud accountancy. We are Sage One Certified Advisors...**

This same story can be presented in a quite different way, with the prospect playing the leading role. I've reworked it so the focus is on the reader and the message is more benefit-led.

Are you an ambitious business owner that wants to achieve your objectives more rapidly? At Profit & Loss Accounting we can help you to gain better control of your finances, providing a more accurate and timely view of exactly how your business is doing and allowing you to take more informed decisions with greater confidence. We also help you to improve the operational efficiency of your finances, save you valuable resources, time and money as well as ensuring everything is compliant.

Here's another example:

Tenon & Mortise is a privately owned British furniture manufacturer located in Wood End. With over 30 years' experience we produce the widest choice of design-led sofas, chairs, tables and storage solutions that offer the very best combination of quality and value for money. Using traditional techniques, fine materials and the incredible imagination of a talented team, we have progressed to become market leaders in our field.

This could be turned around into a story where the reader feels more involved.

What is home to you? Getting the whole family around the dining table for a Sunday roast? Curling up with a good book on the sofa or a night in with a few close friends? The place you dream about when you are stuck at work and the clock stands still on Friday afternoon? It's happy memories, cherished occasions, fleeting moments. It's the heart of everything that's most precious to you...and it's not complete without Tenon & Mortise furniture.

Here's a third example:

**Wood End Hall is a truly unique wedding venue set in ten acres of private parkland. The house boasts traditional ornate features to grace your special day. Our experienced events team provide truly exceptional service that is every bit as personal and individual as you are. With tailored aspects created right down to the very last detail we'll take care of everything.**

There is nothing technically wrong with this description, but it can be made more engaging by framing it around the happy couple and putting the emphasis on the benefits rather than the features.

**A wedding is a supremely theatrical occasion where you direct your own unique love story. With you and your partner centre stage, and family and friends playing the supporting roles, you write your own script. Wood End Hall provides one of the most idyllic and romantic settings imaginable, with expert staff to take care of those little details that make such a big difference. The stage is set for a day you'll fondly remember for a lifetime.**

Give the reader the starring role and you'll immediately draw them in. They start to see how your brand could become part of the story which matters most to them – *their* story.

## Key points to take away

Given the challenging market conditions you need to do everything you can to enhance your brand story.

- Understand the difference between reality and perception – make your offering as good as you can but also work on improving the perception by telling the brand story in a way that emphasises the benefits.

- There's a difference between the bare bones of a story and the way it ends up being told – take advantage of this fact to make your story as remarkable and powerful as you can.

- Make the prospect the hero of your story – that way it becomes *their* story.

# 8. Adding the X factor

Study the world's biggest and most successful brands and you'll see they have followed the process I've shared in this book. They are clear about their features and benefits. They understand exactly who they are talking to and what these people want to hear. They know precisely how they are positioned in their marketplace relative to their competitors. And they have distilled all that down into a powerful and compelling proposition.

Look more closely still and you'll realise that they've also taken full advantage of the fact that, as I explained in the previous chapter, there's a difference between the basic storyline and the final expression of it. The story they start out with and the story they ended up with is hugely different – it somehow got much bigger and better in the telling. In other words, they exaggerated. They added something extra that makes it more remarkable, more dramatic, more memorable and more irresistible – an X factor that amplifies the effect.

Is it possible to do the same with your story? Yes and no. Some of those X factors are prohibitively expensive and therefore beyond the budget of most brands. Others, however, are freely available – and you should exploit them fully. Let's take a quick look at some of the ways the world's best brands have enhanced their stories. There's much you can learn from them – as well as a couple of approaches that even the smallest businesses can usefully exploit.

## Expensive X factors

The biggest brands have a host of challengers. They are constantly looking for a way to get an edge, a means of making their story even sharper.

A quick way to do this is by hiring a celebrity to become a brand ambassador. Omega watches feature George Clooney, Daniel Craig/James Bond and Nicole Kidman in its marketing – the Omega story is instantly supercharged by injecting the star's story into the mix. Tag Heuer does the same with Leonardo DiCaprio, Cameron Diaz and Brad Pitt. In fact most of the top watch brands, each one struggling to differentiate itself in a crowded marketplace, attempts to gain a perceived advantage in the glamour stakes by playing this game of celebrity one-upmanship.

In almost every market you'll find brands importing additional cachet and interest by grafting a celebrity story onto the one they started out with – Kendall Jenner and Pepsi, David Beckham and H&M, Roger Federer and Nike, Serena Williams and Hewlett-Packard.

A further development of this, and a way to introduce added drama, is to link your product story with some kind of expedition story. Omega watches, as well as being endorsed by George Clooney, went to the moon with NASA astronauts. Rolex watches accompanied Sir Edmund Hillary and Sherpa Tensing to the summit of Everest in 1953. Sports sponsorship is a further extension of this same approach, hence Red Bull and Formula

One, Louis Vuitton and the America's Cup and Barclays and the Premier League. Then there's product placement in films and television shows – FedEx in *Cast Away*, Kodak Carousel in *Mad Men* and Manolo Blahnik in *Sex and the City*. All these approaches are essentially the same – make your brand story bigger and better by adding someone else's, or by slotting yours into theirs.

Another way to import additional interest and ramp up the appeal is to change the set, the scenery and the location. Car brands have been doing this for years. Most vehicles don't go anywhere more exciting than a housing estate in Wolverhampton or a hold-up on the M6. In ad-world their favourite habitats include the Atacama Desert, Table Mountain, Monument Valley, LA in the year 2029 and the moons of Jupiter – anywhere, in fact, that is not reality.

Loads of brands do this – a recent John Lewis Christmas commercial featured an old man on the moon, Coors Lite stars Jean Claude Van Damme atop a snow-capped peak and Boden shoots its latest collections everywhere from Cornwall to Mauritius.

Then there's music – a great way to give a potentially flat story a bit of a boost. Think Coca-Cola's 'I'd like to Teach the World to Sing', Yeo Valley's rapping farmers and Cadbury's 'Gorilla'.

Shooting in exotic locations or adding a great soundtrack are just two options amongst many that loosely come under the heading of 'production values'. This is shorthand for 'let's throw a ton of money at the idea to make it look a lot bigger than it really is'. So, you can use expensive computer graphics to turn a Citröen into a breakdancing Transformer, tip a trillion coloured balls down a vertiginous street in San Francisco to launch a new Sony HD TV, or just do Disney with animated cats, dogs or snowmen. Others go totally Hollywood. A great example is the Lynx/Axe commercial for male grooming products that starts in the ice age, hops to the Roman Empire on the day Vesuvius erupts, then recreates the Arabian Nights, fast forwards to the Wild West, before speeding through Victorian London, the sinking of the *Titanic*, a dressing station in the First World War and a 1960's protest march, eventually arriving in the present day. Our frustrated hero, reincarnated many times, finally cheats death in a spectacular traffic accident worthy of a major disaster movie, and gets the girl.

So, those are just some of the ways that brands with money to burn can take a relatively mundane offering and turn it into something a bit more awesome. Most brands, however, simply cannot afford to pull these stunts. The good news, however, is that there are a couple of approaches, also much used by market leaders with deep pockets, that are yours for considerably less.

## Inexpensive X factors

Instead of outspending your competitors you can out-think them.

I've been stressing the importance of psychology, of understanding what your target audience wants and of doing the best possible job of relating your offer to your prospects. Now we need to pull all these threads together and see how they combine at the point where people make their buying decisions.

This will reveal a simple way to make your brand story more appealing, without having to spend a fortune on celebrities, locations or elaborate production techniques.

## Needs and wants

Most people like to think they are not susceptible to the wiles of marketing folk. They also fondly imagine they make their buying decisions, especially for bigger and more expensive purchases, in a way that is considered and logical. However, having spent many years both as a consumer and as a marketer, I'd say that most of us are far more suggestible and pliant than we realise. I'm also convinced that logic plays a much lesser role in the process than we're aware.

A character in Oscar Wilde's *Lady Windermere's Fan* famously remarks 'I can resist anything but temptation.' The same holds true for most of us. How many people get into trouble by doing something they know is wrong, impelled by an urge that gets the better of them? Whether it's taking a second slice of cake, or grabbing one more bargain when the credit card is maxed out, we have all said 'yes' when our head was saying 'no'.

This points to the fact that there's a difference between our 'needs' and our 'wants'. You may not strictly *need* a Mulberry handbag or the very latest iPhone or Sky Sports…but you *want* them. The line 'naughty but nice', used to great effect to promote fresh cream cakes in the 1980s, is a classic example of an advertiser encouraging the prospect to give in to temptation against their better judgement.

Needs are logical, wants are not – and our buying behaviour suggests that we are less creatures of reason than slaves to our desires.

## Head, heart and below

Smart marketers understand this, one minute appealing to our reason and the next switching approach to tempt us with a bunch of feel-good factors, or feel-bad factors, to make their offer harder to resist. As a copywriter I find it helps to have a mental picture of the target audience as just that – a target. I can aim for the head, the heart or lower still.

Think of a great novel or a film and there's so much more going on than mere plot. The creators don't just present a series of events, but touch people on many levels by playing on their deepest fears, their highest aspirations, their most heartfelt desires and their most basic impulses. It's the same with successful brands – the marketers ruthlessly target your senses, your insecurities, your dreams, your instincts to make you *feel* something and then to use those feelings to move you in the direction they want. As eminent neurologist Donald B. Calne has observed 'Emotion leads to action while reason leads to conclusions' (2000).

It's hard to be definitive and prescriptive about human behaviour, but I think we can safely say that much of the time we make our decisions based on feelings, then justify those feelings with logic. We don't need to replace our car with the latest model. But it would make us feel good on a number of different levels. So we tell ourselves things like 'The emissions are lower, so I'm being a good global citizen', 'It has more safety features, so I'm taking better care of my family' and 'It's more fuel efficient so I'll actually save money.' In truth we just want to impress our friends and neighbours!

So, successful brands usually have more than one storyline going on at a time – a logical one, plus a sensual, emotional, spiritual or even a sexual one as well. As Bill Bernbach once advised, 'You can say the right thing about a product and nobody will listen. You've got to say it in such a way that people will feel it in their gut. Because if they don't feel it, nothing will happen.'

## Let's get tasty

There's also an old aphorism, oft repeated by copywriters, that you need to 'sell the sizzle, not the sausage'. You can see this at work with most food and drink brands – they invariably use words and pictures that make the mouth water. For instance, commercials for Bacardi, Coke, Guinness, vodka, cider and lager nearly all feature the obligatory 'pouring shot' to get the taste buds tingling.

## Add some taste value

Let's say you are offering cream teas. You could have a plain shot of two scones with a pot of tea and dishes of jam and cream. But it needs to look delicious, possibly with a suggestion of a sunny English garden in the background – it's not *just* food you are selling, but a mood, a moment, a memory and an experience.

What's more, although the right image may be worth a thousand words, a few carefully chosen phrases will certainly help to paint an equally appetite-whetting mental picture. Instead of merely stating that 'cream tea is served in the conservatory' you could make the description more appealing by laying on the language a bit thicker:

*That most delightful of British repasts, traditional afternoon tea, is served in the sunny conservatory, overlooking the croquet lawn. Delicate finger sandwiches, accompanied by a glorious array of cakes and delicacies, are served with a selection of speciality teas. You'll also be treated to freshly baked home-made scones with lashings of thick Devonshire clotted cream from our local dairy and rich strawberry jam prepared with fruit from our own gardens.*

Which tea would you choose?

Taste is just one of five senses, and there are brands that make an appeal to the others – for instance, fabric softeners to touch, air fresheners to smell, beauty products to sight and audio products to sound. If you decide your brand story could be enhanced by an appeal to one or more of the senses, then you'd be foolish to ignore this opportunity.

## Can I interest you in some sex?

Another famous adage is that 'sex sells' – and almost every product category from cars to jeans, ice cream to cigarettes has employed this tactic. One of the more successful and appropriate instances is Lynx/Axe. John Hegarty explains in his book, *Hegarty on Advertising*, how his agency went about devising a brand story aimed at post-pubescent teenagers. It was clear these consumers, as well as struggling with over-productive sweat glands, were also 'Awash with testosterone and the desire, as they say in the US, "to lock down some tail"'. The 'Brand's appeal, therefore, is very simple: you're not going to lock down some tail if you smell like a hog on heat.' The consumer is the hero in a series of commercials where a very ordinary lad becomes extraordinarily attractive to the most nubile girls imaginable.

Should you use sex to sell your brand? To answer that, follow the process I've given you, decide on your proposition, then ask yourself whether using sex is appropriate – will it enhance your story or detract from it?

## Sexy is sometimes obligatory

Let's say you run a shop and website selling upmar-ket lingerie. Your free and expert bra-fitting service is a major selling point, the logical benefit being that the right combination of cup size and back measurement makes customers feel more comfortable whilst also ensuring that their other clothes fit and hang better. However, it's also true that those who spend a lot of money on underwear probably do so because they want to look good when taking it off! So, if your brand story only sells the prosaic and practical benefits of well-fitting and well-made lingerie then you are almost certainly missing a trick – a degree of sensuality and seductiveness is also called for, both in the imagery and the language.

If you are selling widgets to design engineers, financial products to savers or any form of professional services, then appealing to sexual appetites is clearly not going to help – in fact you'll almost certainly turn prospects off. However, if you are selling fashion, beauty products, fragrances or even chocolate and soft or alcoholic drinks, a little bit of sex might be just what's needed. There are two points I'd make. First, it's a judgement call. And second, it's about how you do it – something I'll discuss further in the next chapter.

## Emotional rescue

As well as appealing to the senses, or sexing it up a bit, brands can target what might broadly be termed the emotions. They've always done this, to an extent, but in recent years this tendency has become increasingly pronounced.

John Lewis adopted their 'Never knowingly undersold' proposition in 1925. It was a prosaic price promise and for almost a century they did little to add to it. However, in 2007 they created a whimsically charming Christmas TV commercial – and never looked back. Each successive seasonal offering has unashamedly tugged on the heartstrings with cute kids, kooky music, adorable animals and extra-large helpings of nostalgia, saccharine and schmaltz. Never knowingly undersold occasionally makes an appearance, but is always secondary to the unabashed assault on the emotions.

Sainsbury's has followed a similar path. In 1882 its first grocery had a sign reading 'Quality perfect, prices lower'. A series of different slogans followed, with 'Good Food Costs Less at Sainsbury's' running from 1959 to 1991. They played around with a few variations in the years that followed, but the emphasis was generally on good old quality and value. Most recently they've adopted 'Live Well for Less', which still encapsulates value but with added feel-good factors such as health and wellness. This then culminated in their 'food dancing' campaign, which is all about the joy of food. It's no longer about making the most of your money but making the most of your life, the ultimate benefit being an entirely emotional one – happiness.

Tesco has gone the same way. Since 1993 they've had the 'Every Little Helps' line, an understated message about savings. They've recently introduced their 'Food Love Stories' campaign which features supposedly real people and their favourite recipes for 'sharing the love' with partners, family and friends. Again, the brand story has moved from a cold and logical price-driven proposition to stories that are unashamedly emotional and heart-warming.

Marks & Spencer has taken exactly the same tack for both food and clothing with their 'Spend it Well' campaign. The company says their intention is to reposition themselves as an enabler of a life well lived. Their launch commercial includes almost all the X factors I've noted – great music (David Bowie), special effects (woman defying gravity and a cloud of clothes), some raunchiness, dramatic locations and even a homage to the Hollywood classic, *Thelma & Louise*.

You can see this trend in almost every sector. Successful brands still have a logical storyline for consumers but they are increasingly loading these with emotions, feelings and sentiment. Even in the B2B sector, where you might expect buyers to make their decisions based on logical criteria such as performance, price and return on investment, brands regularly make a power play for feelings.

'No one ever got fired for buying IBM', a line the company introduced in the 1970s, is a great example of a simple and compelling emotional proposition that derives its power from harnessing the kind of fear that stalks every executive.

Since then countless B2B brands have moved beyond a story that's purely logical. That's because logic takes all of them to the same place. 'We save you time, we save you money and you can trust us' may be accurate, and loaded with benefits, but it doesn't differentiate a brand from competitors. And it certainly doesn't get the prospect's heart racing any faster. Faced with this situation it's no wonder so many B2B marketers play the emotion card.

## UPS has no USP – but it has love to share

You can't get much more logical than logistics, but in 2010 UPS launched their 'We Love Logistics' campaign. It featured lots of heart shapes – trucks parked in a heart formation, boxes with hearts on them, and a heart-shaped symbol, incorporating an arrow, standing in for the word 'love' in the strapline.

It was shot everywhere from Venice to New York, London to Tokyo. It featured the song, 'That's Amore', originally sung by Dean Martin but rerecorded for UPS by Nadia Ackerman.

The lyrics, rewritten from the original, are stuffed with tangible features and benefits that give the business buyer good logical reasons for preferring UPS. If you want to hear them in full you can watch the commercial online. It sells synchronised supply chain capabilities, their tracking system technology and the fact they support just-in-time production. It also has different messages for different types of people within the buyer's organisation (remember what I said about that in Chapter 3?) – some are aimed at the head of IT or production but there are others about carbon footprint, profits and share price for the CEO, chief financial officer (CFO) and shareholders.

They've even used digital animation in multiple scenes with arrows and lines mixed with live action to show the smooth movement of goods, to add clouds of love hearts and even to feature itemised tracking codes for each package. It's all wrapped up with a reassuring promise of peace of mind. You could even argue that the music, and the shot of the pretty girl hugging her UPS delivery man at the end, succeeds in making supply chains sexy. They added every X factor in the book, and threw truckloads of cash at it – the only thing missing is George Clooney!

You can therefore spice up your brand story by appealing to the senses, adding a little romance and by pressing all the available emotional buttons. With a bit of creativity all three can be achieved relatively inexpensively, so they are within reach of even the most cash-strapped brand.

The first two approaches are only appropriate in certain situations. However, an appeal to the emotions is something that *every* brand, from the IT start-up to the niche insurance provider, the micro-business selling handmade jewellery to the medium-sized provider of consultancy services, the local further education college to the 20-person business specialising in bespoke adventure holidays, should incorporate in their brand story. It's just too good an opportunity to miss.

## Key points to take away

- There's an element of exaggeration in all great brand stories – they're enhanced by the inclusion of some X factors.

- Marketers like to boost their stories by adding celebrities, locations and 'production values' – but these ingredients are too expensive for most brands.

- People make their buying decisions based on their feelings, then justify with logic – if you design your story to play on their feelings, prospects find it harder to resist.

- Some brands can enhance their story by appealing to the senses.

- Other brands can enlist the power of sex to spice things up.

- All brands should include an emotional dimension – so make sure you target some of your story at the heart.

People don't buy your widget, your app, your code, your smart phone, your music player, your homemade cupcakes, your fresh flowers, your candles, your music, your computers, your front row seats, your business-class flights, your graphic design, your printing, or your coaching.

They buy how it makes them feel.

The story is your advantage.

Bernadette Jiwa

# 9. *Emotion* – it's what moves people

Emotion is such a powerful, motivating force in any buying decision, and tugging on heartstrings is so effective, that I've devoted a lot of space to discussing it.

Throughout the book I've been leading up to this point by directing you to the need to employ psychology alongside technology, to understand your target audience, to relate your offering to the buyer by stressing benefits – many of which are not merely logical but sensual, instinctive or emotional.

Hopefully you'll now agree with me that playing on the prospect's feelings is an essential element of any brand story that successfully punches above its weight.

## The broom handle and the pin

Imagine I'm standing a few feet in front of you holding a pin in my hand. If I throw it at you, even with all my strength, it will bounce off – the point is sharp, but it doesn't have sufficient weight to go in. However, if I fix the pin to the end of a broom handle, it's a very different story. Put emotional weight behind your logical points and they'll achieve much greater impact!

Having got this far you should now understand how the process I've shared will help you to use emotion in a way that enhances your story, making it more engaging, persuasive and distinctive.

Having said this, some examples may be beneficial. Four earlier ones, although being used to illustrate slightly different points, show how a relatively dull story can be given greater emotional resonance – the example of the mobile bar company in Chapter 1, the furniture company and the wedding company in Chapter 7, as well as the description of the cream tea in Chapter 8. But here are some more for good measure.

## Risk management software

Back in the 1990s a client of mine asked me to help him pitch for the launch of a new risk management software product developed by a small tech company in Silicon Valley's Palo Alto.

We created several different concepts and flew out to present them in California. It was a two-day trip, the first of which involved sitting in a small room with walls entirely lined with whiteboards covered in equations, diagrams and algorithms. Every 40 minutes a different person came in and gave us their version of the brief – background, functionality, features, benefits, target audience, competitive analysis. By 6 pm we were totally overwhelmed with technical detail, exhausted, confused, but sure of one thing – the concepts we were due to present the next day were way off beam.

I awoke at 4 am with the words of the vice president northern hemisphere rattling around my head. In our session with him he had urged us to 'Find the buyer's pain.' He had encouraged us to focus on the fact that the prospects, risk managers, were stalked by fear. These guys lived on the edge, pushing to the extreme to gain competitive advantage over rivals, but at the same time trying to avoid going too far and toppling over. I realised he was right. Forget how the product works, skip all the technical features and benefits, and just scare the hell out of people – they'd be begging us for all the details if we spooked them enough.

I made myself a coffee and wrote a handful of headlines. We presented these to the board, in biro and on cheap paper, a few hours later. They bought every single one and we won the project ahead of some huge US agencies. The launch was successful and the company was sold a few years later for a very large sum of money.

Here's a small sample of those headlines:

**It's a dog eat dog world. Which dog do you want to be?**

The copy started with the subhead: 'You'll be a Chihuahua in a world of Pit Bulls if you don't make the right decisions, right now.'

**It's time for lunch. Who's it going to be today?**

The copy started with the subhead: 'You'll be at the top of the menu if you don't make the right decisions, right now.'

**To move down the food chain simply turn the page.**

The copy started with the subhead: 'Your competitors will eat you alive if you don't make the right decisions, right now.'

John Lewis, Sainsbury's, Tesco, Marks & Spencer and UPS all use positive emotions to move people – but fear is an equally powerful motivator. What's more, this example shows that a highly logical product, that crunches numbers for those calculating business risks, can still be sold by aiming a stab at the heart and a punch to the guts.

## Holidays of a lifetime

Halcyon create bespoke travel itineraries and exclusive holiday experiences tailored to your individual needs. Other aspects of the offering include exceptional personal service, meticulous planning and attention to detail. They also provide inspired ideas from experienced hospitality experts who have amazing contacts all over the world. However, these are all features, and somewhat prosaic.

When I wrote the first page of the brochure I therefore expressed them in more poetic terms, using language designed to stir the senses and make the heart beat a bit faster. I consciously added emotional value and weight:

**Rediscover the days of wonder**

**Halcyon harks back to the golden age of travel, when personal service was the order of the day, faraway countries were still shrouded in mystery and ancient cultures kept their secrets close. We specialise in creating bespoke itineraries for connoisseurs of the exotic, the exclusive and the sensual. Because nothing gives us greater satisfaction than sharing the places we love with those that truly appreciate them. If you are hungry for adventure, romance and pleasure then welcome to the latest edition of the Halcyon Passport – let your imagination off the leash as you are introduced to some of the most sensational destinations on the planet. The world may have shrunk over recent years but inspiring, authentic and unique experiences still await those eager to take the road less travelled.**

The next page goes into more detail of what the service includes, but the approach is still highly emotive, starting with:

**Life is a once-only experience. Made up of fleeting moments that become lasting memories – so there are certain days when everything has to be absolutely perfect. Your wedding, your honeymoon, a special anniversary, a romantic break, a family holiday, a gathering of close friends – these are the events that shape your life, investing it with meaning and value.**

## Free-range camping

A friend of mine, Jules, had three fields where occasionally he let friends camp. Gradually he opened his fields to the public and started adding a few facilities. The atmosphere, however, stayed very relaxed and informal. People loved it for this very reason – most other campsites had loads of rules and were highly regimented.

When Jules finally decided he needed a website he asked me to help write it (petruthpaddocks.co.uk). Going through the brand story process I've shared with you, he and his team came up with the proposition 'free-range camping'. I then set about capturing, and expressing, what free-range camping *felt* like. I described it as:

**A live-and-let-live place where there are refreshingly few rules, kids can be kids, campfires are encouraged, music and bad singing are not a problem and people feel free to wander round making new friends. That's what we mean by free-range camping – and we love it.**

The area furthest from the entrance is the Chill-out Field:

**Through the gate is the Chill-out Field. The clue's in the name. Pitch your tent where you like, get a pile of logs, light your fire, crack open a few beers, singe some sausages, drink more beers, get the guitar, invite the neighbours over, have your own fiesta, or whatever. It's just somewhere you can escape and be yourself, with your family, your mates, your kids, your partner or just on your own.**

Kids are welcome to run wild:

**There are so many rules and regulations these days that kids have a really hard time just being kids.**

**Petruth Paddocks is a PC-free zone – they can run and shout, climb trees and hide in the hedges, fish for tadpoles in the rhynes (what we call ditches in Somerset), kick a football about, clamber over the k\*\*\*\*\*\*\*d old Land Rover in the Chill-out Field, take a ride on the back of the quad bike with Jules, get covered in dirt, make some new mates, and even scrape their knees. Fun is good and play is great – all we ask is that you use a bit of common sense.**

This part of the world has lots of campsites, in much more scenic locations and with far more extensive facilities. So, we had to get a bit creative, and instead of worrying about the competitive weaknesses we played to the strengths. The story evoked the experience, the feelings of freedom, fun, friendships and family.

It worked. In 2014 they welcomed over 10,000 guests – a 500 per cent increase on the previous year. What's more, leading booking site, pitchup.com, confirmed that the site came from nowhere to become their best-selling campsite in the UK, beating over 1,000 sites across the country by a very healthy margin indeed. There were a whopping 1,388 bookings through pitchup.com between January and September 2014, exceeding the nearest competitor by a massive 23 per cent.

Hopefully these three examples will help you to appreciate how to move people more effectively by increasing the emotional quotient in your brand story.

## Key points to take away

- Whatever kind of business you are in be sure to add emotional weight to your story.
- Emotion adds impact .
- Emotion combined with logic means you make sharp points that go in.

A smile is the shortest distance between two people.

Victor Borge

# 10. Wit – the ultimate weapon of mass persuasion

There's one more way you can ratchet up the power of your brand story. Like appealing to the emotions, you can do it without breaking the bank – so even the smallest business can employ it. In one way it's an approach aimed at the head. But it creates emotion – so it probably falls into the general area of emotional intelligence.

What I'm talking about is wit. And it's the nearest thing I know to a brand story silver bullet – one trick that'll get your message through when all else fails.

## The missing ingredient

As my career progressed I got more ambitious. Over a period of 18 months I arranged appointments with London's top creative directors. They critiqued my work, then sent me on my way. I used their feedback to improve my portfolio before booking more interviews. I eventually got a job at Young & Rubicam, at that point the world's largest ad agency, working on big brands such as Heinz, Colgate-Palmolive, Dairy Crest, Suchard, Air Canada and British Gas. All those months of criticism and rejection from the sharpest brains in the business were invaluable, and free.

The most astute insight I received was this. The creative director looked at one of my layouts and said 'There's something missing from this ad.' Being a bit cocky, I replied 'It has a picture, a headline, body copy, a call to action, strapline, logo, contact details – what *more* do you want?!' There was a pause before he said 'Wit.' He was right.

You probably think I'm referring to wit in the sense of 'humour'. And you might also think I'm referring to the subject of 'tone of voice'. You're partly right, on both counts – but what I have in mind is much bigger than either.

## Tone of voice

When I tell people 'I'm a copywriter' they used to say 'Oh, slogans?' Now they reply 'Ah, tone of voice!' Tone of voice is much in vogue at present – you'll seldom find a set of brand guidelines without it being covered.

Tone of voice is less what a brand says about itself and more *how* it says it – the sound, modulation and colour of the language. The tone a brand adopts will amplify the story and make it resonate on an emotional level with prospects. The marketers may decide the tone should be fun, serious, honest, professional, friendly, scientific, passionate or humorous – tonality comes in many flavours. Tone is important because it evokes feelings – and as I've explained at length every brand story needs an emotional dimension.

It's therefore vital to find a pitch that's 'in tune' with your story. Everyone cites Innocent Drinks as a good example – the product itself is innocent (not guilty of using added sugar, concentrates or any 'funny business') and so is the tone of voice (clear, simple, real, truthful, nothing artificial – 'written the way we talk to our friends'). Likewise, if you are a health and safety consultant, your tone should probably be relatively serious and authoritative. If you are hiring out bouncy castles it needs to be fun and playful. A bakery producing sticky cakes, gooey eclairs and mouth-watering yum yums can afford to be naughty, devilish and thoroughly indulgent. The tone and the story need to harmonise with each other.

## Tone of voice – a note of caution

A lot of brands and marketers are lazy. They've not bothered to go through the rigorous analytical process I've shared with you. Instead, they've taken a shortcut and just adopted a tone of voice to disguise that they really don't have much of a story. The secret of Innocent's success was not the loveable tone of voice but the fact they developed exactly the right kind of distinctive drinks at precisely the right time. The tone helped, but without the unique qualities of the product it would have led to disappointment and failure.

So, whatever you do, don't fondly imagine that tone of voice is a substitute for a story of substance. As I noted at the beginning, too many marketers treat the message as irrelevant. They leave it until the last minute then get someone to pad the website, advertising, literature and social media feeds with bland content that merely fills a space. They then add a superficial sprinkling of tone of voice, to tart it up. There's a big difference between a story that's been properly constructed by a brand architect, and one that's just a confection whipped up by the branding equivalent of an interior decorator.

Wit, although it strays into tone of voice territory, goes beyond it. And, although the effect can be comic, it is also far more than mere humour. The *Oxford English Dictionary* defines wit as 'the capacity for inventive thought and quick understanding; keen intelligence' and as 'a natural aptitude for using words and ideas in a quick and inventive way to create humour.' It's about mental playfulness, creativity, sharpness, agility. It might make you laugh, but often it is cerebral, and produces wry food for thought. One of the best definitions I've ever come across is 'a smile in the mind', from the book of that title about wit in graphic design, by Beryl McAlhone and David Stuart.

### Ten great reasons why wit is incredibly powerful

- It gets attention. Wit can trick people into noticing something they would otherwise have missed or ignored.

- It is rewarding. There's a payoff, and that means people forgive the fact they've been tricked or intruded upon.

- It disarms people and breaks down barriers. Even if a person is closed off and wants to be left alone they find it hard to resist.

- It defuses tension. It's a great way to make people relax and become more receptive.

- It makes people smile and kick-starts relationships. As Victor Borge says 'A smile is the shortest distance between two people.'

- It gives pleasure, it is welcomed, it gets likes and shares. Witty people are popular, people enjoy their company and people enjoy introducing them to others.

- It is admired. People respect witty individuals.

- It is interactive. Wit demands some effort on behalf of the audience, drawing them in and creating involvement.

- It credits people with intelligence. The audience has to be smart to 'get it' and there's a reward when they achieve it – this makes people feel good about themselves.

- It buys you forgiveness. There are certain things that you normally couldn't get away with – but say them with wit and people love you for it.

Brands are like people – the whole process of 'branding' is about taking inanimate products and services then finding ways of humanising them. Imagine how successful and popular your brand would become if it had all the attributes listed above!

It'll be easier to see what I'm talking about if I give you some examples.

## The Economist

This periodical has a very distinctive brand story and tone of voice devised by legendary copywriter David Abbott. One of the earliest *Economist* ads he wrote simply had the line: 'I never read *The Economist*' in large type, followed by, in smaller type, the words 'Management trainee. Aged 42.'

As Abbott explains in Crompton's *The Copy Book*:

What is potentially a banal positioning ('read this and be successful') is made acceptable and convincing by wit and charm. Directness has its place in advertising but so do subtlety and obliqueness. Things you can't say literally can often be said laterally. (Crompton, 1995)

## Lynx/Axe

In every commercial a very ordinary young lad becomes instantly irresistible with a quick spay of deodorant or squirt of shower gel. Hordes of Amazonian women compete in a race to reach him, sexy angels fall from heaven to sin with him, a girl starts throwing off her clothes when their trollies collide in the chiller aisle of the supermarket and drags him across town to bed, a string of gorgeous women excuse his men-behaving-badly traits and indulge his most tiresome laddish tendencies in their eagerness to sleep with him.

Clearly all these stories are absurd, as is the line 'Spray more, get more.' But it is all done in such a witty tongue-in-cheek way that we suspend our disbelief and surrender ourselves to the entertainment.

So, wit works. Big time. And you don't need a Lynx/Axe-sized budget to pull it off.

## A business card worth its weight in gold

Twenty years ago, when I started freelancing, my target audience was design agencies. They loved brushing me off with 'We don't need a copywriter – a picture is worth a thousand words.' After hearing this for the nth time I had some new business cards printed. These were folded to create four business card-sized pages. On the back were the words *Jim O'Connor. Copywriter*, and my contact details. On the front, in a classic Garamond typeface, was the message A PICTURE IS WORTH A THOUSAND WORDS. Inside, right across the double-page spread, in big graffiti-like type, was scrawled:

# Bollocks

I had intended it as a bit of fun, but it worked so well I've had it reprinted regularly for over two decades. People ask me, 'Have you got any of those cards left?' or 'Can I have one for my friend?' They proudly tape it, with the 'b' word on display, at the side of their computer monitor. I can be walking down the street, minding my own business, and someone will wave and shout 'Bollocks'. My wife has even got used to being greeted as Mrs Bollocks. And I regularly get calls from people I gave the card to five or even ten years ago. A little stroke of wit, and fun, has provided serious income for me, month after month, year after year.

## Posters still loved by the punters

About 15 years ago I did some posters for the gym where I was a member. I liked it because it was full of nice, ordinary people, not knucklehead bodybuilders or leotard-clad bimbos. So, the proposition and strapline became: *for people, not posers*. Above this ran a huge headline. One was:

**Ordinary people. Not Steroid types.**

Another was:

**Meet. Not Meat.**

And:

**Feel like somebody. Not some body.**

Simple. Very cheap to produce. And still running – originally on the back of buses but now on the wall of the gym.

## Not all accountants are grey

You don't have to be big to be funny. Psyche Coderre, interviewed by *The Guardian*, says she chose her name at the age of 16 to reflect her 'growing interest in alternative music and subculture. I loved The Cult, Sisters of Mercy, The Cure and The Psychedelic Furs. The Goth image just appealed to me' (Williams, 2014).

After 20 years dressed in black, and with purple hair, she had become a veteran of this scene. So when she passed her accountancy exams she saw no reason to change her style.

She called her business Death and Taxes, with the strapline 'Keeping you in the black'. She explained that:

I set up Death and Taxes to challenge the 'boring accountant' stereotype and help small businesses. My clients include mainstream businesses and others, such as comedians, a burlesque dancer, a punk band, etc. Most have come via recommendations and they don't have a problem with my name or appearance. (Williams, 2014)

She adds that 'Not looking like a "typical accountant" has attracted customers running alternative businesses and media interest has attracted others' (Williams, 2014).

Wit is priceless, and affordable. A brand story without it is seriously missing a trick.

### Key points to take away

- Wit is the most powerful weapon in your armoury – and it is one that even the smallest brand can afford to deploy.

- Tone of voice is important – but it's no substitute for substance.

- Wit can be humorous, but it's more than that – much more.

- Your brand will become much more successful if you tell its story with wit – for ten very good reasons.

Never do anything yourself that you can hire someone else to do, especially if they can do it better.

**Bill Bernbach**

# 11. Get some professional help

The brand story preparation process I've shared with you is something you can complete yourself. But appealing to the senses, introducing sexiness, pressing emotional buttons and attempting to be witty all takes skill – get it right and your brand will fly, but get it wrong and you'll come down with a nasty bump.

You almost certainly need to enlist the help of a small collection of professionals – a graphic designer, a web designer and a copywriter, at the very least. You might find them working together in an agency, or you might need to source them individually and create a project team. I'd give you two pieces of advice.

First, don't choose any of these professionals without seeing examples of their work. If they don't have any it's a sure sign they are either inexperienced or embarrassed at the quality. Marketing people are great at talking the talk – but you need to see proof that they can deliver. What's more, interrogate the work to make sure they can think and work strategically. Pick several of their previous projects and get them to explain the objective, the target audience, the proposition and why they approached the task in the way they did. You need to make sure they were following a well thought-out plan and that they delivered something appropriate and effective. Also check whether they managed to add any of the X factors we've discussed, including emotion and wit.

Second, make sure you have your story sorted and pinned down before you brief anyone. And get the copywriter involved before you let the designers loose – the message needs to shape the design, not the other way around.

Finally, a word of reassurance. If you are disappointed to discover that you still need some professional help, even after reading this book, then I'd say this. At least you know how to prepare your story and give them a proper brief. Not only will this set them off in the right direction and give them all the information they need to complete the job, it will also provide you with a template against which to judge the work they come back with. This will save you a huge amount of time, confusion, frustration and money. It will also put you out ahead of all those competitors who are not in this happy position.

---

### Key points to take away

- Adding X factors like sensuality, sexiness, emotion and wit to your brand story takes skill – you probably need professional help.

- Choose professionals who can demonstrate their competence by showing you completed projects.

- Don't brief these professionals until you have your story properly organised.

- Using the process outlined in this book will prove hugely beneficial.

# Your brand story checklist

- Have you listed all your features and benefits?

- Do you have your target audience clearly defined, along with the key motivating factors that influence their buying decisions?

- Are you clear on how you are positioned in your marketplace and what your strengths, weaknesses, threats and opportunities are?

- Have you created a single-minded proposition that is motivating and differentiating?

- Are your features and benefits organised in a way that substantiates your proposition?

- Have you made the most of your story by adding all the X factors that are available to you – sensuality, sexiness, emotion and wit?

A brand is the most valuable piece of real estate in the world: a corner of someone's mind.

John Hegarty

# Bibliography

Arden, P. (2003) *It's Not How Good You Are, It's How Good You Want To Be*. Phaidon.

Calne, D. (2000) *Within Reason: Rationality and human behavior*. Penguin Random House.

Carnegie, D. (2006) *How to Win Friends and Influence People*. Vermilion.

Crompton, A. (1995) *The Copy Book: How 32 of the world's best advertising writers write their advertising*. RotoVision.

Dobrow, L. (1984) *When Advertising Tried Harder: The 60's, the golden age of American advertising*. Friendly Press.

Hegarty, J. (2011) *Hegarty on Advertising: Turning intelligence into magic*. Thames & Hudson.

Jiwa, B. (2013) *The Fortune Cookie Principle*. The Story Telling Press.

Maslow, A. (2013) *A Theory of Human Motivation*. Wilder Publications.

McAlhone, B. and Stuart, D. (1996) *A Smile in the Mind: Witty thinking in graphic design*. Phaidon.

**Bibliography**

Ogilvy, D. (1983) *Ogilvy on Advertising*. Pan books.

Reeves, R. (2015) *Reality in Advertising*. Widener Classics.

Toffler, A. (1970) *Future Shock*. Bantam Books.

Trott, D (2008) 'Simplify and Exaggerate'. Dave Trott's Blog. Available at: http://davetrott.co.uk/2008/11/simplify-and-exaggerate/ Accessed: 8/6/2017.

Williams, M. (2014) 'Why daring to be different can be good for business'. *The Guardian*. Available at: https://www.theguardian.com/small-business-network/2014/dec/05/daring-to-be-different-good-business Accessed: 05/12/2014.

# About the author

Jim O'Connor has worked in marketing and sales for about 40 years, developing a profound interest in the art of creating successful brand stories.

After graduating with a degree in English Literature he sold advertising space for the Newcastle *Evening Chronicle*. He then set up and ran a light haulage business, as well as a market stall.

This was followed by jobs at several Tyneside ad agencies before he was headhunted by a relatively new company called Saatchi & Saatchi. After several years working in their Charlotte Street offices as an account manager he moved to an agency in Bristol, this time in the creative department.

Several years later he landed a job in London as a copywriter with Young & Rubicam, working on major brands like Heinz, Colgate-Palmolive, Dairy Crest, Suchard, Air Canada and British Gas.

He then started dividing his time between freelance copywriting, and recruiting, training and managing a team of over 400 agents for a major direct selling organisation. About ten years ago he began concentrating all his efforts on marketing communications, developing his Stories that sell consultancy.

He now works with a variety of different companies and brands – from household names to micro-businesses, software developers to finance providers and boutique hotels to leading retailers. For further details visit storiesthatsell.co.uk or read his blog storiesthatsell.co.uk/blog.

# Other Authority Guides

The Authority Guide to
Networking for Business Growth:
How to master confident, effective
networking and win more business

Rob Brown

**You *can* master the mysterious art of networking.**

Overcome all your networking fears and learn how effortlessly to build
and leverage the powerful connections you need to enhance your reputa-
tion, raise your profile and win more business. Networking expert Rob
Brown will coach you on all the essential skills that will help you meet new
people, create new leads, open up opportunities and grow your business
– confidently and effectively.

# The Authority Guide to Pitching Your Business:
# How to make an impact and be remembered – in under a minute!

## Mel Sherwood

**Make that first impression count.**

Create success and secure more business with a powerful pitch that really packs a punch. Avoid all the common pitfalls and learn how to boldly and succinctly explain what you do in less than 60 seconds. In this fast, focused *Authority Guide* Mel Sherwood shares her expert knowledge to give you the skills you need to prepare and deliver a professional pitch with authority, confidence and passion.

# The Authority Guide to Writing and Implementing a Marketing Plan: A step-by-step manual to make you a smarter marketer and maximise your business profits

## Ambrose and Jo Blowfield

**Get the most from your marketing with an expert plan that really gets results.**

Written especially for small businesses, this *Authority Guide* shows you how to write and execute your marketing plans efficiently and accurately. Ambrose and Jo Blowfield will help you create plans using proven, affordable marketing tactics for both digital and traditional strategies. You'll have a year-long marketing plan that is structured, well thought out and targeted to your ideal clients, allowing you proactively to promote your business.

We hope that you've enjoyed reading this *Authority Guide*. Titles in this series are designed to offer highly practical and easily-accessible advice on a range of business, leadership and management issues.

We're always looking for new authors. If you're an expert in your field and are interested in working with us, we'd be delighted to hear from you. Please contact us at commissioning@suerichardson.co.uk and tell us about your idea for an *Authority Guide*.